Shelley Holmes
Animal
Trainer

Michaela Morgan

Illustrated by Dee Shulman

D0232202

OXFORD

UNIVERSITY PRESS

Chapter 1

Shelley Holmes was bored again.

So was her best friend, Kelly

and so was Dustbin, her dog.

sigh

It was the middle of the long holidays.

There were weeks more of...

...nothing to do.

They were all watching an old video and wishing.

Then Shelley had one of her ideas.

'I bet WE could do that!' she said.

'I'm not swinging on a trapeze or walking on a high wire,' said Kelly, 'or juggling fire or having knives thrown at me!'

'I mean I bet we could train animals,' said Shelley.

'**I** could do it! I could be a world famous *animal* trainer.'

I'd wear feathers
in my hair...
high heels...
sparkly tights.
I can see it now...
my name in lights.'

'Hmm...' said Kelly.

said Dustbin.

'It will be EASY
PEASY,' said
Shelley.

'It can't be that hard.
How hard can it be to
make a pony run in
a ring

or a chimp wear a hat...

or get an
elephant to stand
on three legs?

We could do that, no problem!
No problem at all.'

Kelly thought about it for a bit.
Then she said, 'Well, we do have one
problem...'

'Hmm...'
said Shelley.

Dustbin woke up.

Chapter 2

Shelley and Kelly dragged Dustbin down to see their friend, the vet.

'We want to learn how to train Dustbin,' said Shelley.

'That's a GOOD idea,' said the vet.

'You could train him to stop eating my waiting room.'

'Now let me see... There are lots of different sorts of training.'

Why don't you go along and see what you think of these...

She gave them some leaflets.

SMART HEART ♥

AGILITY TRAINING

Has your dog got the heart of an athlete?

Come along to our weekly sessions at: 118 High Jump Pounding

SHEEP DOG TRAINING

Sheep Farm
Sheep Wash

FLYBALL

A new playful training

Fun fitness for dogs!

Bounce Lane

OBEDIENCE TRAINING

Teach your dog to obey your every command.

Sportshall
2 Stern Road

13

'That's the one for us!' said Shelley. 'I want to train Dustbin up to be a star. And I'll become a world famous animal trainer.'

But then the vet pointed out some of the more important details on the leaflets.

So they decided to go for the
Obedience Training in the Sports
Centre.

'It's a start,'
said Shelley.
'Come on,
Dustbin.
You'll love it!'

Chapter 3

The Sports Centre was very busy.
  There was Fun and Fitness for the
Over-40s.

There was a disco upstairs.

There was swimming in the pool.

The Brownies' Tea Party was in the small hall,

and in the big hall... dog training.

There were dogs of all
shapes and sizes all waiting
for a chance to show how
obedient they were.

Some of them were old
friends.

There was Colin the
collie and his owner.

There was Fifi the poodle
and her owner.

There was Bully the
bulldog and his owner
and Spotty the Dalmatian
and his owner and...
rather a lot of others.

YAP! YAP!

RUFF

They had all been before
– except Dustbin.

They were all eager to trot to heel
– except Dustbin.

They were all waiting quietly
– except Dustbin.

'Let's go,' hissed Kelly. 'Dustbin can't do any of this.'

But Shelley was determined.

'Keep your dogs on their leads,' said the teacher, 'and reward him or her with regular treats – a bit of sausage, a biscuit, a doggy chocolate drop...'

All the owners had come
prepared with smart leads,

special chains,

whistles
and clickers,

pockets full of
treats,

and lots of spare
treats which they kept
in bags around the hall.

Shelley and Kelly were not quite
so well prepared.

Dustbin's lead was slightly
chewed, and they hadn't
thought about bringing
any doggy treats.

'I've
got some
raspberry
bubble gum,'
whispered
Kelly. 'We
could try
that.'

'We'll start with something very easy,'
said the teacher.

Walking forward
... Normal pace...
start now!

All the dogs trotted off
smartly and earned praise

Good dog!

Oos a ickle
tweasure then?

and treats.

But Dustbin
was less
than keen.

What? No
choccy drops!

23

All the other dogs were given treats.
But not Dustbin.

'When he does as
he's told he gets a
treat. And not
before!' said the
teacher.

All the dogs turned around smartly and walked back sensibly.

But not Dustbin. He was more interested in treats.

So he didn't get a reward, and Shelley was not pleased.

The next thing the
owners and dogs were
asked to do was...
weaving.

'Take your dog, on its lead, and
weave in and out of the others. Go!'
    Most of the dogs were quite
good at this,

but not Dustbin.

So Dustbin still got no treats,
and he was getting quite hungry.

'I think Dustbin is
a bit peckish,' Kelly
whispered.

Peckish?
I'm famished.

'He'll be good at the next thing,' said Shelley. But he wasn't.

He didn't get a treat for walking to heel.

He didn't get a treat for sitting

or for lying down.

Dustbin was one disappointed dog and Shelley was one unhappy animal trainer. 'I can't be expected to become a world famous animal trainer working with Dustbin. He's hopeless!'

By the end of the session Shelley and Dustbin were getting desperate

and when the teacher said, 'We will now let each dog off the lead for the recall exercise,' Kelly had a feeling that all would not go well.

'Let's get out of here,' Kelly hissed. But Shelley was determined.

I can make him do it! I know I can!

Shelley took Dustbin off his lead and Kelly held him, tightly, while Shelley walked to the other end of the hall.

'When I give the order,' said the teacher looking at Kelly, 'you release the dog.

Then,' and here she looked at Shelley, 'you give the recall signal.'

'Then the dog,' and here she glared at Dustbin, 'the dog will run straight to you and sit by your side.'

The teacher gave her commands.

First to Kelly:

Then to Shelley:

Then to Dustbin:

Dustbin went.
He went like the wind.

He went into the
corner to snaffle the
sausages.
He went through
everyone's pockets
trawling for treats.

OY!

HEY!

!CHOMP!

SLURP

CRUNCH!

He went into bags
and boxes chomping
the chocolate drops
and then...
he kept going.

MUNCH!

STOP THAT
DOG.!!!

He went into the small hall to join in the Brownies' tea

Slobber!

and he even went upstairs to the disco...

where he ate the snacks,

drank the drinks

and even danced a couple of dances.

'I refuse to have that dog in this class,' said the teacher.

'He'll have to go down into the puppy class.'

'Sorry,' said Shelley.

'Sorry,' said Kelly.

'Perhaps this isn't the sort of training for us. We'll try somewhere else... sorry...'

 # Chapter 4

Dustbin looked downhearted.

And so did Shelley. 'I give up,' she sighed. 'I'll never be able to train him.'

'I suppose… we could try… the agility training,' Kelly suggested.

'**YES!**' said Shelley. 'Dustbin will be great at that. And it **is** the cheapest. This is the way to our fame and fortune!'

Kelly was not so sure.

She was even less sure when she heard what Dustbin was expected to do.

'What the dogs do,' said the teacher, 'is simply climb these steps,

walk this plank,

jump over this fence,

go through this tunnel,

over the see-saw and through the hoop.'

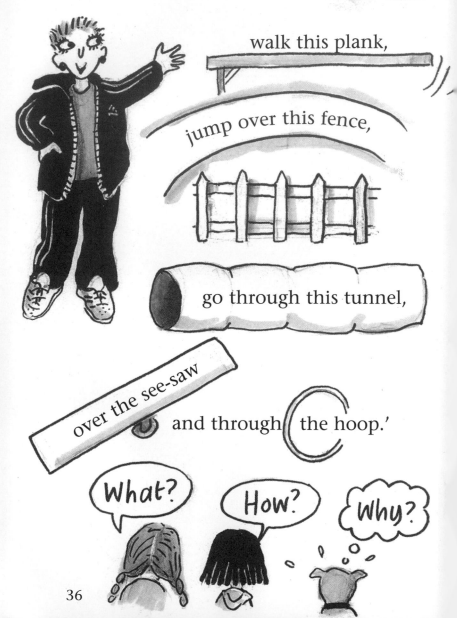

What? How? Why?

'And when they get to the end we give them a treat.'

Oh, now I see!

Dustbin did his best.

He walked the plank,

jumped the fence   sort of,

AAAH!

went through the tunnel,

37

over the see-saw,

oops!

and through
the hoop.

'Now he deserves a reward,' said the teacher.

'So… we pat his head and tell him he's a good boy!'

After that Dustbin went on strike.

Even Shelley was fed up with the training.

So was Kelly

and ... so was Dustbin

Treats! I want treats.

'Maybe I won't be a world famous animal trainer after all,' Shelley was thinking. 'Maybe I'll be something more sensible, like ...'

...an astronaut

But then Shelley heard something
very interesting...

Chapter 5

Kelly managed to get Dustbin's name on the register.

Shelley had very high hopes.

Kelly had very deep doubts

and Dustbin had
… a very rumbly tummy.

The afternoon was spent
grooming the dogs
for stardom.

They were all

bathed,

brushed,

fluffed up

and smoothed down.

In the end they were all sweet-
smelling, glossy-coated and smart –
well, nearly all.

Shelley and Kelly did their best with
Dustbin but it wasn't easy.

He'd eaten his brush.

BURP!

Soon Mr Beilsperg, the
film producer, and his
team arrived to put the
dogs through their paces
and to choose the

 new star for the
Krunchkins dog food ad.
The dogs and their
owners lined up for the
first test.

This was the beauty competition.
'We want to select a good-looking
dog,' said the film producer.

The next test was the fitness test.

The next test was the intelligence test.

'For this test your dog has to get to the box, press the pad, release the ball, catch it and bring it back.
O.K. Go!'

Dustbin did his best.

At least he got to eat the ball.

'Dustbin has no chance. Let's
get out of here,' said Kelly.

But there was one last test.

'This is the most important test of
all... and the easiest,' said Mr Beilsperg.

'We simply pour out a bowl of
delicious Krunchkins and we film your
dogs eating it and looking happy.'

The film producer poured out the Krunchkins.

It looked like sawdust with a few beans and peas thrown in.

Bully's owner muttered:

No dog in its right mind would eat that!

Fifi looked at it and sniffed.

No, No, zey cannot be serious!

Colin's collie wouldn't even go near it.

Bully looked at it and bit the hand that fed him.

'All the dogs have failed,' said the producer and his team... and then they saw Dustbin.

First he nibbled, thoughtfully.

Then he licked, appreciatively.

Then he chewed – thoroughly –

and then he scoffed the lot and beamed.

'That dog has a superb appetite!' said the producer.

'He's the one for us!'

HOORAY!

So all the next week Kelly, Shelley and Dustbin were treated like stars and Dustbin was given bowls and bowls and bowls

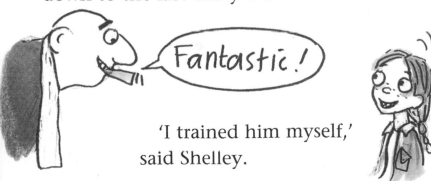

to eat and he ate every single one right down to the last dusty crumb.

Fantastic!

'I trained him myself,' said Shelley.

By Friday, the filming was finished.

'That's it,' said Mr Beilsperg. 'The film is made! Thanks for everything. Now we have to do the testing for the toilet duck.'

Shelley was DELIGHTED.

'There!' she said to Kelly. 'I knew we could do it.'

But behind her,
Dustbin was just
finishing off another
tasty little snack.

About the author

This is my second story about Shelley, illustrated by Dee Shulman.

I had a dog that was very much like Dustbin.

He could eat anything (toys, books, shoes, his own dog bowl).

He could jump in the air and twirl.

But he never learned to obey a simple command like 'Stay!' or 'Sit!'

Perhaps I should have taken him to dog school?